A Little Round Island in the Middle of the Sea

Bob Broshears

Illustrated by

Sierra Mon Ann Vidal

To order additional copies of this book, contact:
Xlibris
844-714-8691
www.Xlibris.com
Orders@Xlibris.com

ISBN: Softcover   978-1-6698-1412-2
        Hardcover   978-1-6698-1413-9
        EBook   978-1-6698-1411-5

Print information available on the last page

Rev. date: 04/18/2022

A Little Round Island in the Middle of the Sea

Bob Broshears

Illustrated by
Sierra Mon Ann Vidal

For
Ruth Romero
and
Alene Gray Broshears

with
Aloha for Kathleen Viernes and
Christa DeRaspe McLeod

It is only a little round island in the middle
of the sea, yet how beautiful it is.

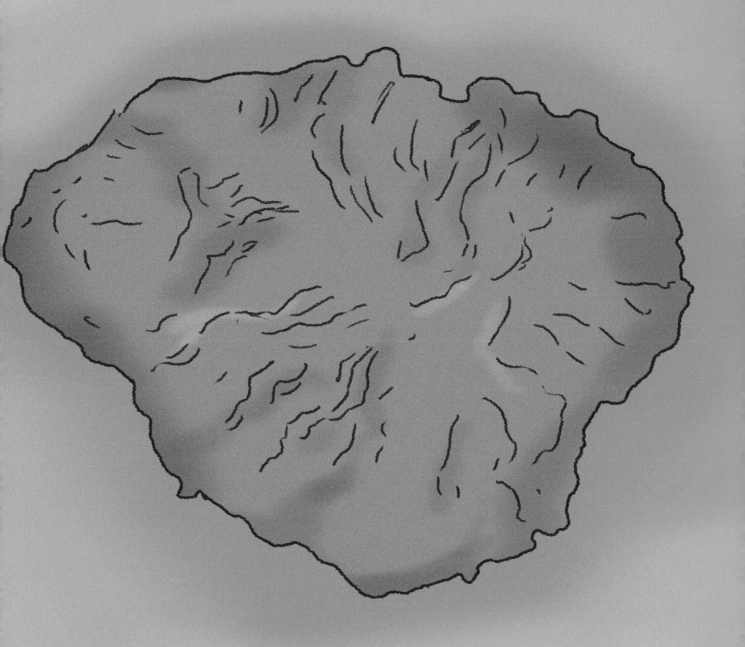

Once upon a time, there was a deep blue
ocean so vast that even a high-flying bird
could not see the end of its waters.

Miles beneath the wind-swept surface, molten rock emerged from the sea floor, and over many years the hot rock grew upon itself until one day it found air above the waters.

Higher and higher the molten rock grew,
forming a little round island in the middle
of the sea.

The high island captured rain from prevailing trade winds, and with those winds came seeds of life. First grasses and later tall plants, then inevitably the majestic birds. The land prospered in seeded green fields, festivals of birds, and an explosion of life from the sea.

As the land continued to rise, rain carved deep canyons from the lava tops, feeding fertile grasslands around the island.

A few large geese blown from far away enjoyed abundant food in the lovely grasses of the island. Absent the wolf and the bear of their homeland, they found peace, fearlessness, and prosperity.

Smaller birds, their light weight held easily aloft for thousands of miles in the winds, discovered new homes in the misty mountains. In the air cloaked in fog, only the most colorful birds could arouse mates, and over the millennia the honeycreepers evolved. Only those with the longest and thinnest of curved beaks could extract nectar from mystic mountain flowers.

From small northwest islands albatross arrived on the little round island in the middle of the sea. Pairs of these large birds danced.

They danced with their heads held high into the sky, they danced clicking each other's beaks, and they danced to celebrate the little round island.

One parent stayed on the egg, while the other soared hundreds of miles at sea in search of food for its mate. After the chick emerged, both parents flew for days, now with three mouths to feed.

The young albatross grew into the longer days, flight feathers replacing down, until finally she fledged, following her destiny above and on the sea. It was a time of magnificent and timeless beauty.

And then a new element entered. From the southern horizon, tree poles with hala sails emerged from the sea, and below those sails, a wooden platform mounted on double hulls.

Humans!

The first people of the island embraced a fresh paradise. They celebrated the island in reverent songs and joyful dances for centuries to come.

But with human arrival, the little round island would change forever.

Some of the changes would enhance the island's beauty. Some would not. Those changes are our common human legacy.

The future of the island remains forever in our hands.

It is only a little round island in the middle of the sea, yet how beautiful it is.

Printed in the United States
by Baker & Taylor Publisher Services